LYNN FREEMAN OLSON

Audience Pleasers

A special collection of 14 favorite solos for piano students at the early elementary to elementary levels

BOOK 1

Early Elementary to Elementary

The magic of a piano solo by Lynn Freeman Olson is irresistible. His music delights, inspires and thrills both teachers and students alike. Now, in three books, Alfred presents a collection of some of Lynn Freeman Olson's AUDIENCE PLEASERS. Turn the page, and let the music of Lynn Freeman Olson enchant you and your students.

Alfred

Indian Celebration

Lynn Freeman Olson

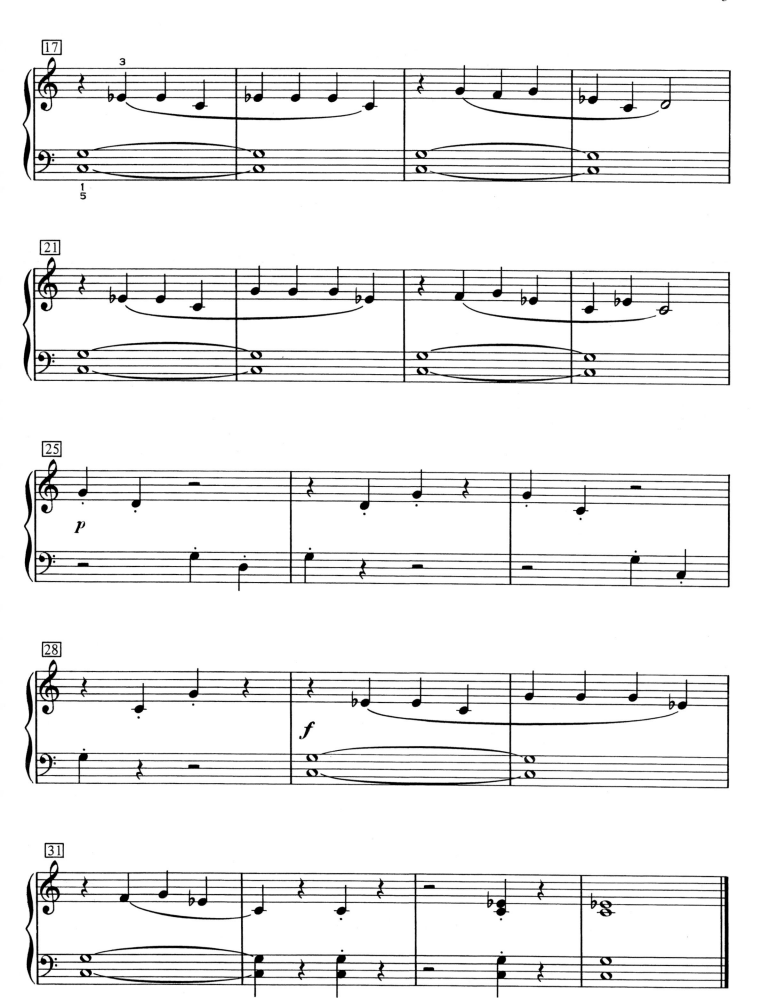

A Happy Secret

Lynn Freeman Olson

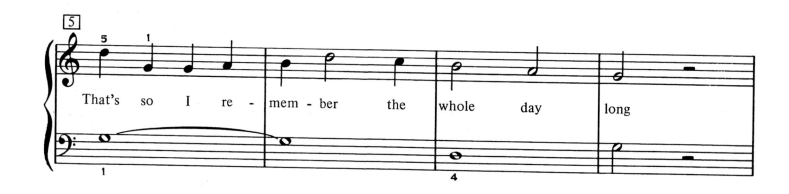

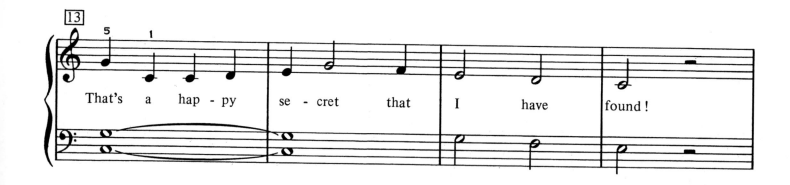

17 *HAPPY MUSIC*

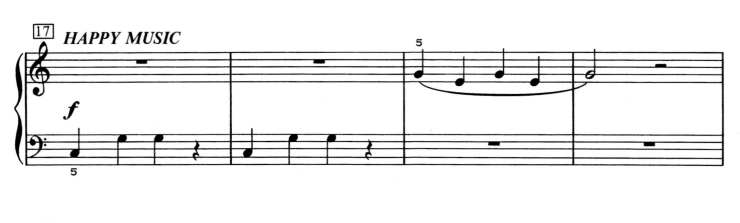

21 *(RH move)*

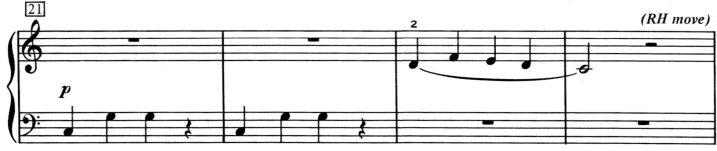

25 *(RH move)*

When I wear a smil - ing face, I share it all a - round!

29

That's a hap - py se - cret that I have found!

33 *A BIG SMILE!*

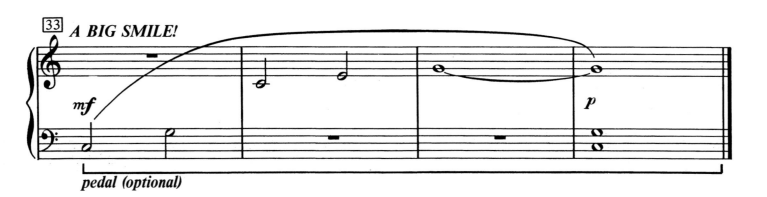

pedal (optional)

Little Bird Lost

Lynn Freeman Olson

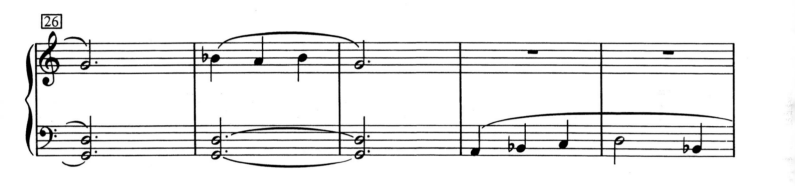

The Sixpence Song

Lynn Freeman Olson

I've got six-pence, yes, it's real-ly true! Jol-ly six-pence,

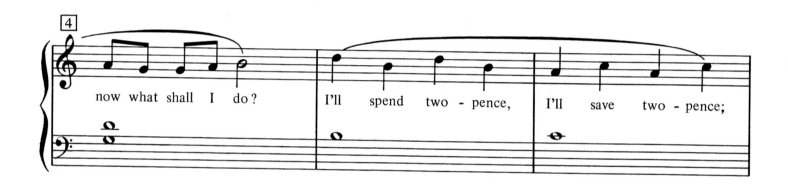

now what shall I do? I'll spend two-pence, I'll save two-pence;

Two-pence left, and they're both for you!

Square Dance Tune

Lynn Freeman Olson

Old-Time Train Ride

Lynn Freeman Olson

Rolling along quickly

The Old Typewriter

Lynn Freeman Olson

Pecking quickly, staccato throughout

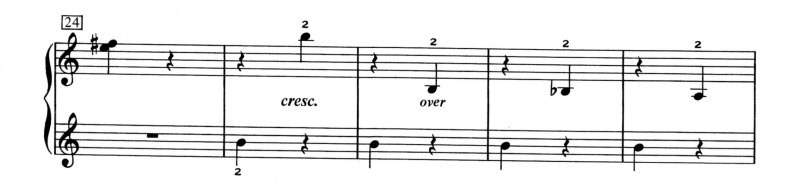

cresc.   over

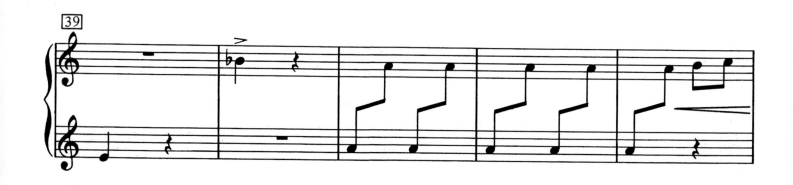

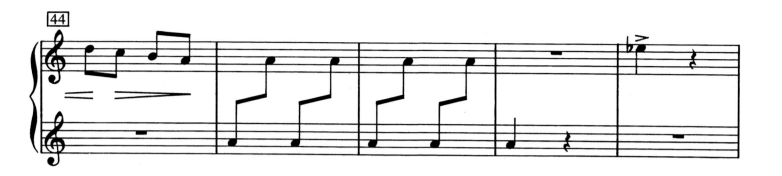

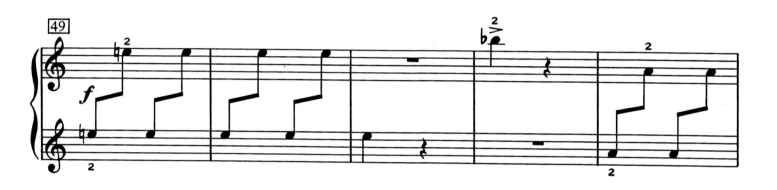

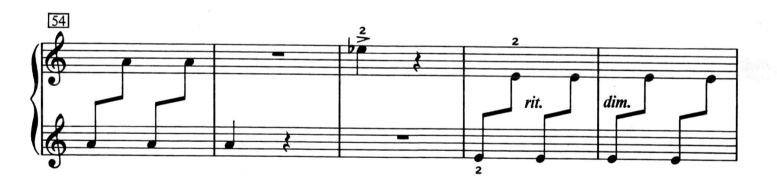

Across the Desert

Lynn Freeman Olson

Blazing Trumpets

Lynn Freeman Olson

Bright and lively

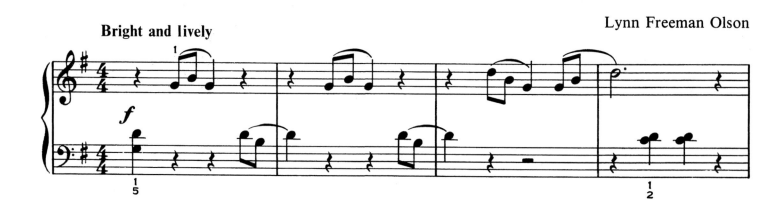

The Rainbow Song

Lynn Freeman Olson

Singing along

It's a rain - y day, Clouds are dark and gray,

Sad face in the win - dow says, "Can't go out to play!"

Watch the chang - ing sky, You'll see, by and by,

Sun - shine will be smil - ing through, Rain - bow rid - ing high!

17 RAIN AND CLOUDS

RAINBOW

Watch the chang - ing sky,

You'll see, by and by,

Sun - shine will be smil - ing through,

Rain - bow rid - ing high!

Star Light, Star Bright

Lynn Freeman Olson
from a traditional song

Ride in the Blimp

Lynn Freeman Olson

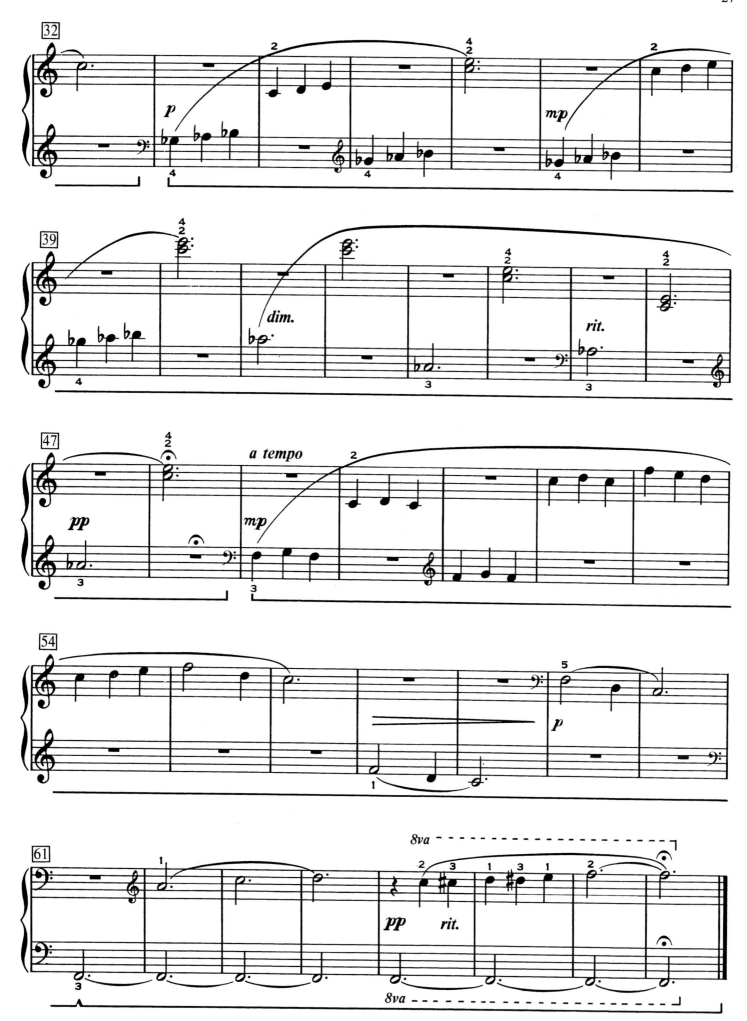

Horse and Rider

Lynn Freeman Olson

Galloping like the wind

Tricky Trampoline

Lynn Freeman Olson